Contents

It's in the post

Nearly every day post arrives on your doormat. Some of it is official and sometimes it's a postcard from a friend. Best of all are the cards and presents you get on your birthday or for Christmas.

Post

Where Does It Come From? Where Does It Go?

Paul Humphrey

Photography by Chris Fairclough

W

FRANKLIN WATTS
LONDON•SYDNEY

This edition 2004

Franklin Watts
96 Leonard Street
London
EC2A 4XD

Franklin Watts Australia
45-51 Huntley Street
Alexandria
NSW 2015

Planning and production by Discovery Books
Editors: Tamsin Osler, Samantha Armstrong
Designer: Ian Winton
Art Director: Jonathan Hair
Illustrators: Stuart Trotter
Commissioned photography: Chris Fairclough

A CIP catalogue record for this book is available from the British Library

Dewey Decimal Classification: 383

ISBN: 0 7496 5255 1

Printed in Malaysia

Acknowledgements
Franklin Watts would like to thank the Post Office Library for allowing the reproduction of the photographs on the following pages: 4, 20, 21, 24, 25, 28 and 29.

Some of your mail comes from somewhere nearby. Some post is national, coming from places a long way from your home. Some is international mail, from another part of the world altogether.

People get in touch with each other by telephone, fax or e-mail, but if you want to send someone a present or a parcel, by post is the easiest way.

Lots of letters
The Royal Mail was set up in 1635. Today, it handles 82 million letters, cards and parcels each day!

Businesses send documents to other businesses and to their customers by post. We receive catalogues and deliveries by post, too. Just how does all this post get to the right place?

5

Starting the journey

Do you have a friend to write to?
What if you wanted to send them some
photographs of you or your house?

You need to write your friend's name,
address and post code clearly on the
envelope. If you are sending a letter,
you can just stick a stamp on the envelope.
But if you are sending something heavier, like
photographs, you should take it to the post office.

Post codes

A post code is a series of letters and numbers used by the Royal Mail. The country is divided into 120 areas.

1. Each area has a code letter or letters. The code for Birmingham is B.

2. Each area is divided into districts which are given a number, like B99.

Paul Watson,
2167 Kentwardine Ave,
Birmingham,
B99 2SP

3. Districts are divided into even smaller sectors and given another number, like B99 2.

4. Lastly, each sector is broken down into streets, parts of streets or even large businesses and factories, which are given two letters, like B99 2SP.

At the post office

The heavier your letter is, the more it costs to send. At the post office your letter is weighed to see how much it will cost to send.

If you want your letter to reach your friend the next day, then you need a first class stamp. If it isn't urgent, you can send it second class. The letter will take one or two days longer, but second class post is cheaper.

You should stick the stamp in the top, right-hand corner of the envelope. If you put it anywhere else, your letter may take longer to get to its destination. Now put it in a post box and your letter is on its way!

Stamps

The cost of the stamp pays to have your letter delivered. Stamps were invented over 150 years ago by Sir Roland Hill. British stamps are the only ones not to carry the name of the country, but they always show a little picture of the king or queen's head.

Collecting the mail

At certain times each day a postal worker unlocks the post box. Every post box has a different key. The letters and small parcels are emptied into a sack and loaded into the post van.

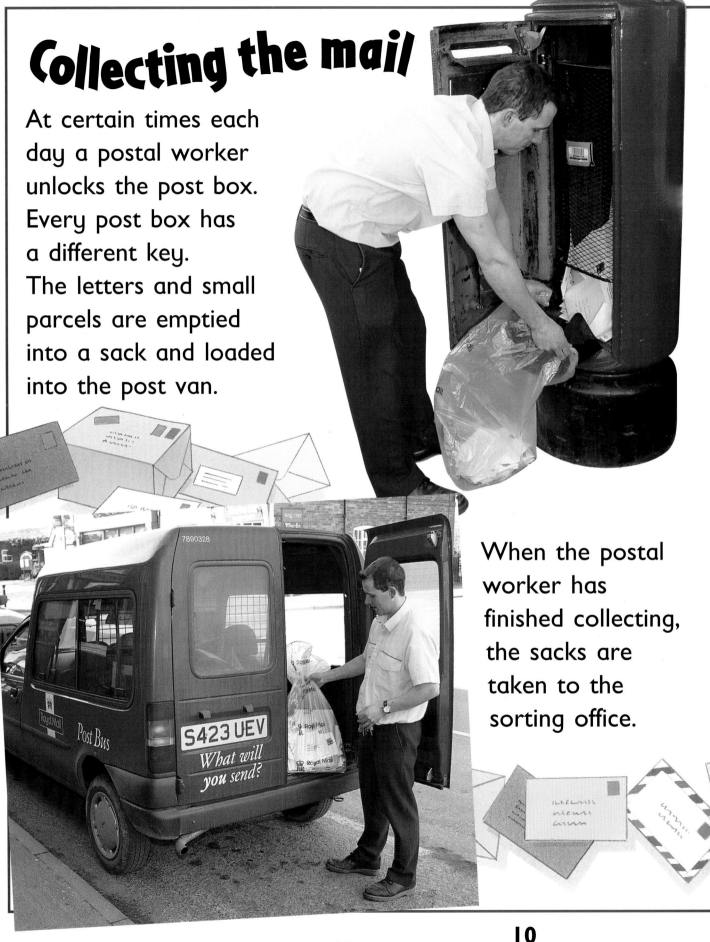

When the postal worker has finished collecting, the sacks are taken to the sorting office.

Post boxes

The first post boxes in Britain were used in 1853. They were octagonal and green.

Look at the letters on the box. The initials tell you who was king or queen when the box was put there.

VR stands for Victoria Regina, or Queen Victoria.
ER stands for Edward Rex or King Edward, or for Elizabeth Regina.
What do you think GR stands for?

The sign on the front of the post box shows the times of the collections from that box. The number in the little window tells you which collection comes next.

At the sorting office

Here letters and parcels are sorted into groups for the different places they have to go. When the postal worker arrives, the mailbags are loaded onto a trolley and wheeled into the sorting office.

Sorting offices

There are 1,500 sorting offices across the country, one in every big town. Some big cities may have more than one sorting office.

The mailbags are emptied onto a moving belt that carries them into a huge machine called an Integrated Mail Processor, or IMP.

First the letters go into a big drum, or 'culler' that turns around, separating the small letters from the larger items. These are sorted somewhere else in the sorting office.

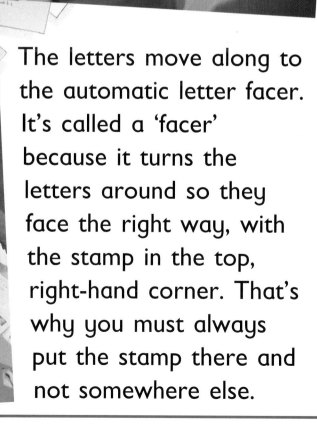

The letters move along to the automatic letter facer. It's called a 'facer' because it turns the letters around so they face the right way, with the stamp in the top, right-hand corner. That's why you must always put the stamp there and not somewhere else.

Postmarks

The automatic letter facer prints a postmark on the letter. This tells you which sorting office sorted the letter and when. Then the machine 'cancels' the stamp, by printing a wavy line over it. This stops anyone using the stamp again.

Royal Mail
Birmingham
Mail Centre
08.03.00
04.33 nm
22700510

Please use the Postcode

39P

The automatic letter facer can also read most printed post codes and some hand-written ones too. If it can read the post code it prints pink lines on the letter. This is a computer code for the post code.

Busy IMP

Sorting offices are busy twenty-four hours a day as an IMP runs all the time, sorting the post. It may be sorting the letter to your friend while you are getting ready to go to bed.

The computer room

What happens if the machine can't read the post code or if you sent the letter without a post code? First, a camera in the IMP takes a photograph of the envelope. The letter is given an 'electronic tag' and ejected from the machine.

The photograph is sent along wires to the computer room where it appears on a screen. The computers contain the post codes from all around the country so the operator types in the right code for the address.

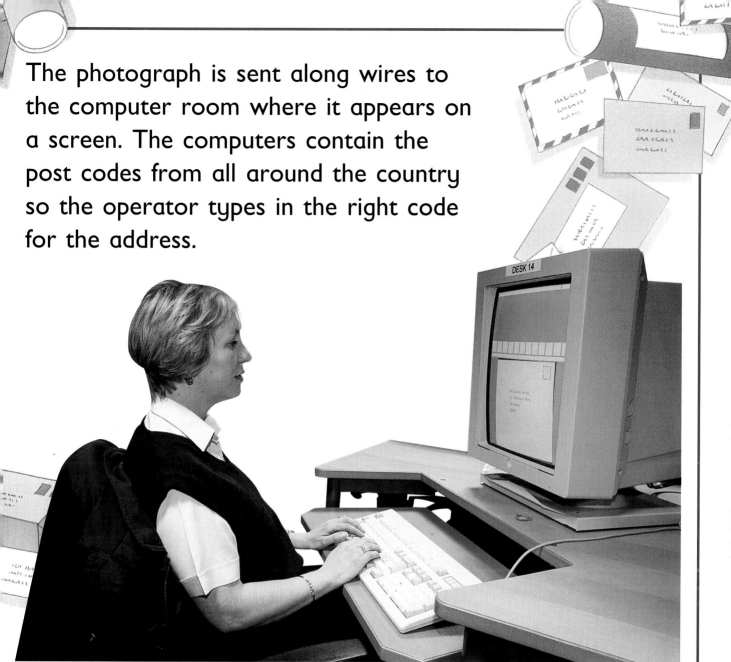

The post code is then sent electronically back to the IMP. Now, when the postal worker puts the letter back into the IMP it recognizes the electronic tag and the correct pink bar code is printed on the envelope.

Sorting the mail

The last part of the IMP is a sorting machine. This sorts all the letters into cities or areas according to their post codes. All the mail for each area is dropped into its own box.

A postal worker empties the letters from the sorting machine into separate mailbags. One of these bags has the letter you posted to your friend in it!

Post for the local area is now ready to be delivered but post for nearby towns and cities is taken there by van or lorry. The mailbags containing post that has further to go usually travel by train.

Bikes to buses

The Royal Mail has a fleet of 29,000 vehicles and 33,000 bicycles. It also has 38-tonne lorries. Together they travel 700 million kilometres a year to deliver our mail. In some country areas post buses (right) carry passengers, as well as mail.

Mail by rail

At the railway station mail is loaded into a mail carriage. Some mail carriages are fitted out as sorting offices. Here the mail is sorted through the night so that it can be delivered early the next morning when the train arrives.

Some post is taken around the country by air. Nearly three million letters are carried in aeroplanes every day!

Underground mail

The streets of London are so crowded that it takes post vans hours to get from one place to another. So London has its own underground system just for mail trains. The mail trains, which have no drivers, run along 35 kilometres of track.

Delivery

Once the mail arrives at a station or airport early in the morning, it is taken to the nearest sorting office. Here, another machine sorts the mail into each postal worker's delivery area.

Postal workers start work long before you are awake. First they put the post into the right order for their round, making sure that the letters they deliver first are at the top of their bag.

Then they either cycle to their area, if it is nearby, drive a van, if it is a big area, or are taken to it, if they can walk the whole route.

Town and country

In the country postal workers may cover a huge area and they usually drive from house to house and from village to village. In a city, with lots of houses, shops and offices, they may only have a few streets to deliver to.

Your postman or postwoman then delivers the mail to your door.

Parcel post

Parcels take a different route. After they are ejected by the IMP, they are taken to another part of the sorting office where they are sorted either by hand or machine. The postal workers cancel the stamps and print the postmarks by hand.

There are lots of sacks with the different post codes marked at the top of each one. Postal workers fill each sack with the mail for that area.

If you are sending a very large parcel you will have to send it by Royal Mail Parcel Force. This is a separate part of the postal service.

International mail

Have you ever sent a letter or parcel to another country? Most overseas letters go by air mail. Parcels can be sent either by air or surface mail – over land and by sea. Surface mail takes much longer to get there than air mail.

Air travel is expensive, so air mail costs more. This is why air mail letters are often written on lightweight paper to make them as light and cheap as possible. The envelopes are light too. They usually have a label with 'Air Mail' and 'Par Avion', on them. (Par Avion means 'By Air', in French.)

AMC SAN FRANCISCO
(U S A)

SFO

At the sorting office, air mail letters are sent in trays or sacks to an international sorting office. Here, the letters are sorted according to country before being put into sacks and labelled. Each label has a code printed on it by a computer. The sacks are then taken to the airport.

In the air

Often mail is carried in ordinary passenger planes, but sometimes it travels in special mail planes. The sacks of mail are put into large metal containers, which are wheeled and loaded into the plane.

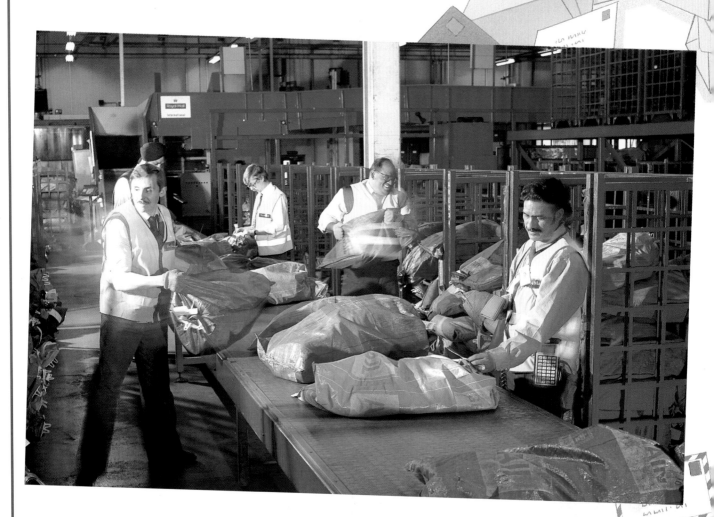

The mail is then flown to its destination. If you are sending a letter to New Zealand, it could be in the air for 24 hours!

When the plane arrives, the sacks are taken to a local sorting office. Here they are sorted according to the local post codes into areas, districts and streets, just like inland mail. The letters are then ready to be delivered.

Glossary

Air mail   Post that travels by air.

Automatic letter facer   A machine that turns letters around to face the right way up.

Culler   A big turning drum that separates smaller letters from larger letters and packages.

Destination The place where something is going.

Inland mail   Letters that are posted to a place in the same country.

Integrated Mail Processor (IMP)   The machine that processes mail in a sorting office.

International post   Post that travels from one country to another.

International sorting office   The office where international post is sorted according to the destination country.

National post   Post that travels to a destination within the same country.

Post bus   A post van that also carries passengers.

Post code   The letters and numbers in an address that help the sorting of post.

Post mark   The printed mark on a letter or package that tells you the date, time and name of the sorting office where it was sorted.

Sorting machine   A machine that sorts letters according to their post codes.

Sorting office The place where post is sorted for delivery.

Surface mail   Post that is sent by land and sea.

Further reading

Burns, Peggy, *Post*, Wayland, 1994

Gibbs, Stephen and Perry, Philippa, *Post Office*, Wayland, 1994

Ramsay, Helena, *Where Does A Letter Go?*, Evans, 1997

Stewart, Alex, *Everyday History: Sending a Letter*, Franklin Watts, 2000

Watson, Carol, *A Day in the Life of a Postman*, Franklin Watts, 2000

Index

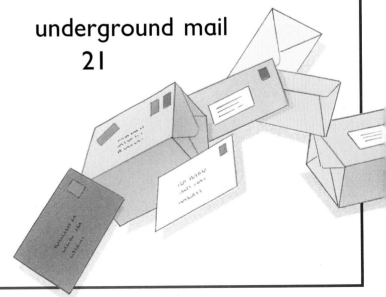